# Kayaking and Rafting

## Paul Mason

Smart Apple Media

Smart Apple Media
2140 Howard Drive West
North Mankato, Minnesota 56003

First published in 2007 by
MACMILLAN EDUCATION AUSTRALIA PTY LTD
627 Chapel Street, South Yarra, Australia 3141

Visit our Web site at www.macmillan.com.au or go directly to www.macmillanlibrary.com.

Associated companies and representatives throughout the world.

Copyright © Paul Mason 2007

Library of Congress Cataloging-in-Publication Data

Mason, Paul, 1967-
Kayaking and rafting / by Paul Maso.
p. cm. — (Recreational sports)
Includes index.
ISBN 978-1-59920-133-7
1. Kayaking—Juvenile literature. 2. Rafting (Sports)—Juvenile literature. I. Title.

GV784.3.M37 2007
797.121—dc22

2007004599

Edited by Vanessa Lanaway
Text and cover design by Pier Vido
Page layout by Pier Vido
Photo research by Naomi Parker
Illustrations by Boris Silvestri
Map on pp. 28–9 by Pier Vido

Printed in U.S.

**Acknowledgements**
The author and the publisher are grateful to the following for permission to reproduce copyright material:

Front cover photograph: Group of people white-water rafting on Salmon River, Idaho, courtesy of PhotoDisc.

Photos courtesy of:
Hein van den Heuvel/Zefa/Corbis/Australian Picture Library, p. 25; BananaStock, p. 27; Brian Bailey/Getty Images, p. 30; Alan Becker/Getty Images, p. 10; Mike Brinson/Getty Images, p. 13; Ghislain & Marie David de Lossy/Getty Images, p. 8; Jeri Gleiter/Getty Images, p. 12; Jock Montgomery/Getty images, p. 21; Chris Noble/Getty Images, p. 22; Vladimir Rys/Getty Images, p. 26; Yellow Dog Productions/Getty Images, p. 14; Istockphoto, p. 16; Attila Balaz/Istockphoto, p. 24; Simon Krzic/Istockphoto, p. 6; Bradley Mason/Istockphoto, p. 18; Michael Olson/Istockphoto, p. 9 (bottom); Piotr Sikora/Istockphoto, p. 23; Mark Strozier/Istockphoto, p. 9 (top); PhotoDisc, pp. 1, 4, 5; Demin Tony/Photolibrary, p. 11; Photos.com, p. 7; U.S. Department of Agriculture, p. 27.

While every care has been taken to trace and acknowledge copyright, the publisher tenders their apologies for any accidental infringement where copyright has proved untraceable. Where the attempt has been unsuccessful, the publisher welcomes information that would redress the situation.

The author thanks Hammy Dallimore for his comments on the text.

# Contents

**Glossary words**

When a word is printed in **bold**, you can look up
its meaning in the glossary on page 31.

# Recreational sports

Recreational sports are the activities we do in our spare time.
These are sports that people do for fun, not necessarily for competition.

You have probably tried some recreational sports already. Maybe you would like to know more about them or find out about new ones? Try as many as you can—not just kayaking. Also try biking, hiking, fishing, climbing, and snorkeling. This will help you find one you really love doing.

## Benefits of sports

Recreational sports give people lots of pleasure, but they also have other benefits. People who exercise regularly usually have better health. They find it easier to concentrate and do better in school or work.

Kayaking does not have to be scary—exploring the coast in a kayak can be lots of fun, too.

# White-water sports

White-water sports take place on fast-flowing rivers. As the rivers rush over shallow places and down steep drops, they make frothy white bumps of water. People use rafts or kayaks to ride on the river as it races downstream.

## Rafting

Plunging along a river in an inflatable raft can be very exciting. Rafts carry several people, so you could try it with a group of friends.

## Kayaking

Kayaking is done in small, narrow boats. Kayaking can be a white-water sport. People also use kayaks to explore lakes, rivers, coastlines, and the ocean surf.

Rafting is done using a tough, inflatable boat.

# Getting started

To try white-water rafting or kayaking, you need a fast-flowing river. Other kinds of kayaking take place on slower-moving rivers, lakes, or the sea.

## Trying rafting

Most people first try white-water sports on an organized rafting trip. After a talk about safety, everyone heads for the river. The person in charge of the boat is called a river guide. The river guide plots the raft's course down the river, and makes sure everyone finishes safely.

## WATCH OUT!

How dangerous is the river you are traveling down? Rivers are graded with a number that tells you how risky they are:

| | |
|---|---|
| Grade 1 | Easy |
| Grade 2 | Novice |
| Grade 3 | Intermediate |
| Grade 4 | Advanced |
| Grade 5 | Expert |
| Grade 6 | Extreme |

Rafting is a great way to try white-water sports with your friends.

Learning to paddle and steer a kayak is easiest on calm water.

## Learning to kayak

The best way to learn to kayak is by going on a course or joining a club. Kayaking is more difficult than rafting. It is important to get some training. Kayaks are easier to tip over, and you are in the kayak alone. You must learn how to paddle and steer your kayak, as well as how to rescue yourself if it tips over.

The best places to learn kayaking are on still, calm waters. Lakes and slow-moving rivers are good places to start. Lagoons, which are sheltered areas of seawater, are also great for your first kayaking trip.

"Everyone must believe in something. I believe I'll go canoeing."

U.S. writer Henry David Thoreau (1817–62).

# Rafts and kayaks

Rafts are specially designed to be able to survive in **white-water rivers**. Kayaks are used in lots of different kinds of water. There are many different types of kayaks.

## White-water rafts

White-water rafts have a very tough skin. The raft's skin is so tough it can scrape over rocks without getting a **puncture**. The outside edges of the raft are inflated, but the floor is not.

White-water rafts are built to be tough so they can endure rocky rapids.

The river guide, who is in charge, sits at the back

Paddlers usually sit on top of the edges, with their legs inside

Short paddles

Safety lines run along the top

# Kayaks

There are many different types of kayaks. They are usually made from solid plastic. You can also get fiberglass, inflatable, folding, and other kayaks. Two extremes of the kayaking world are the white-water kayak and the sea kayak. Other designs are somewhere between these two, depending on what they are used for.

Curves in the nose and tail help the boat turn easily

Paddler's knees fit in here

Paddler sits on an adjustable seat

Short kayak to aid control in white-water

Flat bottom

Small white-water kayaks are easy to turn.

Front storage hatch

Rudder helps steering

High front cuts through waves

Paddler sits here

Rear storage

Long sea kayaks are comfortable and stable on long trips.

# Clothes and equipment

The clothes you need for rafting and kayaking are similar. They keep you safe, warm, and dry.

## Staying safe

Two key pieces of equipment keep you safe: a helmet and a life jacket. The helmet is especially important in white-water, where it keeps your head from being damaged if you fall in. The life jacket brings you back to the surface if you are dragged under.

## Staying warm

Most paddlers stay warm by wearing a wet suit. This keeps the heat in even if you fall in the water. A helmet helps keep your head warm.

In cold weather or water, paddlers also wear wet suit boots and gloves. Some sort of footwear is always useful, in case you end up having to walk on the riverbed.

The right safety equipment means white-water rafters can enjoy the wild water.

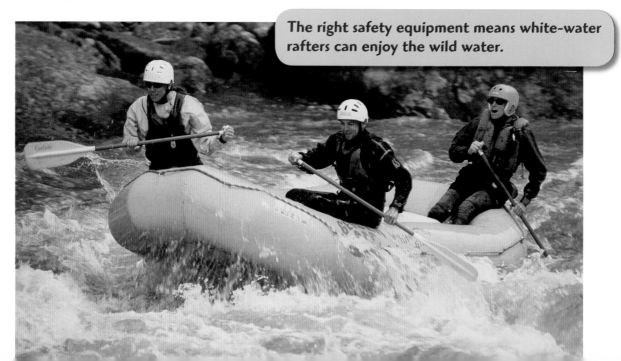

## Staying dry

Even in warm weather and warm water, paddlers usually wear a special top to keep the water and sun off their body. The tops have **cuffs** that can be sealed to keep the water from getting into them.

Kayakers also wear a spray skirt. This is a special skirt that goes around their waist. The bottom edge of the skirt fits around the edge of the **cockpit**. This makes it impossible for water to get inside the kayak.

**Top tip!**

Carry a t-shirt and shorts rolled up in a bag so that you have something dry to wear after a wet paddle.

Paddlers wear special gear to keep them warm and dry.

Paddle

Helmet

Life jacket

Waterproof top with sealed cuffs and neck

Spray skirt

# White-water rafting skills

Your first white-water rafting trip will almost certainly be with an organized group. The instructor, or river guide, will explain how everything works before taking you to the river.

## Teamwork

Everyone on the raft has to work together as a team. If they do not, the raft will go off course, which would be dangerous. The river guide is in charge. All of the other paddlers must follow his or her instructions.

## Organizing the raft

Once you reach the water, the river guide will organize where everyone sits. He or she will put an equal number of people on each side of the raft. The idea is for there to be equal paddle power on each side. The guide sits at the back in the middle.

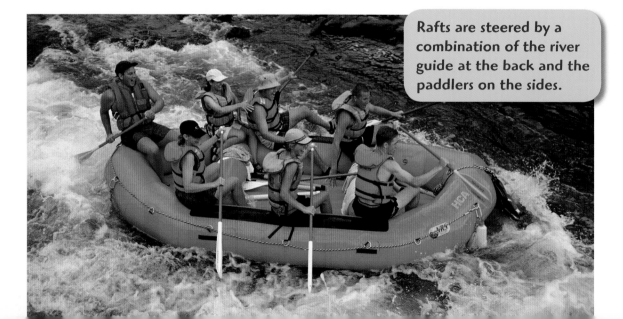

Rafts are steered by a combination of the river guide at the back and the paddlers on the sides.

## Launching

Once everyone is seated, the guide launches the raft, pushing it away from the shore. This usually happens in calm water, to give everyone a chance to get used to paddling.

## Paddling

Once the raft is launched, the river guide gets everyone to practice paddling before the raft reaches the white water. This is to make sure the paddlers are ready to help steer the raft wherever the river guide tells them.

The paddlers sit on top of the raft's sides. They hold their oar with both hands, about shoulder-width apart. To paddle, they twist their body forward, dig the paddle in the water, and pull back.

### Paddling instructions

Guides use instructions such as these to help them steer the raft.

- "Paddle right!" People on the right side paddle, causing the raft to steer to the left.
- "Paddle left!" People on the left paddle, and the raft steers to the right.
- "Paddle together!" Both sides paddle together, and the raft shoots forward in a straight line.

Be sure to keep your weight inside the raft when leaning out to paddle.

Top tip!

Paddle in time with the person in front of you.

# Long-distance rafting

Some rafting trips take several days. The longest trips can last weeks, as the raft journeys down a giant river to the sea.

On a long trip, rafters may have to help portage their raft.

## Planning ahead

A long rafting trip takes a lot of planning. Food, clean water, clothes, tents, and sleeping equipment all need to be packed. They must also be kept dry! Rafters use special waterproof bags for this.

## Portaging

Portaging is the name for carrying your raft or kayak. People usually do this because the river is too shallow or too rough for them to paddle along it.

"Anyone who says they like portaging is either a liar or crazy!"

*Bill Mason, famous Canadian white-water enthusiast.*

# Different landscapes

Long rafting trips usually pass through lots of different landscapes. In hilly country, the raft will go through **rapids**. The banks of the river will be steep, and it might be hard to find a place to **moor** for the night. Other days, the river might flow gently along through flatter landscapes, with plenty of beaches to rest on.

**WATCH OUT!**

Never stop for the night on a riverbank unless you are sure it is safe from floods.

## Technique

### Sleeping by the river

Falling asleep in your sleeping bag beside the river is a great experience. Here are a few tips to make sure you wake up happy in the morning.

1  Make sure your raft is pulled out of the water. Tie it to something solid with at least two lines.
2  Camp as high above the water level as possible, in case it rises while you are asleep.
3  Keep as much gear as possible in waterproof bags.

Make sure your camp is safe and dry before going to sleep.

# Kayaking skills

If you enjoy white-water rafting, you might also like to try kayaking. Kayaking is more difficult, but you can learn on slower, calmer waters before heading off to the rapids!

## Basic skills

The basic techniques of kayaking are:
- getting into the kayak and launching it into the water
- paddling in a way that does not use too much energy
- steering the kayak
- escaping from the kayak if it turns over, and getting back to shore

**WATCH OUT!**

A stopper happens when water gushes over a steep ledge. It hits the bottom, then comes back over itself, making a kind of sideways whirlpool.

The best way to learn these skills is by joining a kayaking club or going on a course. If a friend teaches you, make sure that he or she is a very experienced kayaker.

Plotting a course through white water is a great skill.

# Launching a kayak

Before you can paddle a kayak, you have to launch it.
Usually, this is done either from a beach or from a jetty.

### Launching a kayak

Practice launching your kayak in calm, shallow water.

**1** Put the kayak down in line with the bank, in water that is just deep enough to float it.

**2** Put your paddle onto the deck of the kayak behind the cockpit, with the other end resting on the bank.

**3** Grip the paddle against the edge of the cockpit. Use it to steady the kayak as you get in.

**4** Fasten your spray skirt. If necessary use the paddle to shove yourself toward deeper water.

A kayak paddle has its blades at different angles.

# Paddling

There is a special trick to paddling a kayak. This is because the **blades** at either end of the paddle are usually at an angle of about 80 degrees to each other. You have to turn the paddle each time you do a **stroke** with it. This is done by twisting your wrist and rolling your shoulders as you dip the paddle into the water.

## Using your legs

Your legs have an important job to do while paddling a kayak. Your knees push up against the top of the kayak, while your heels push down. This keeps you from slipping around, and makes it easier to paddle smoothly and powerfully.

**Top tip!**

Long paddle strokes are tiring. Shorter strokes save more of your energy.

18

# Steering

The two basic ways to steer a kayak are forward-paddle strokes and backward-paddle strokes.

## Forward-paddle turn

If you paddle forward on one side only, it will push the kayak the opposite way. So, if you want to steer right, paddle only on the left-hand side. The kayak will turn slowly to the right. This type of turn is best if you want to keep up your speed.

## Backward-paddle turn

Paddling backward on one side of the kayak will turn it in that direction. So, if you want to turn to the right, paddle backward on the right-hand side of the kayak. It will quickly swing round to the right. This type of turn is best if you want to slow down or turn quickly.

# Emergency escape

Kayaks can be unstable and easy to tip over. What do you do if you suddenly find yourself upside down, under water?

## Technique

### Emergency escape

Getting out of an overturned kayak quickly is a skill that could save your life.

**1** Do not panic! The spray skirt has a tag on it in the middle at the front. Pull on this, and the spray skirt will peel back.

**2** Next, roll forward with your head going toward the deck of the kayak.

**3** If necessary, push on the sides of the cockpit. Your body and legs will come out of the kayak.

**4** At the surface, grab the kayak's **carrying toggle** (there is one at each end). This will help you float.

**5** Grab your paddle, then tow your kayak to dry land.

## WATCH OUT!

Always make sure the pull-tag on your spray skirt is on the outside, so that you will be able to get hold of it in an emergency.

## Eskimo roll

The Eskimo roll is a way of getting upright without getting out if your kayak tips over. It is named after the Arctic people who invented kayaks. The water in the Arctic is too cold to do an emergency escape and swim to dry land. People can freeze to death if they are under water for more than a few seconds. Instead, the Arctic people learned to use their paddle and flick their waist to turn their kayaks right-side up again.

Most expert kayakers can use the Eskimo roll to get upright again if their kayak tips over.

**WATCH OUT!**

You must be able to do an Eskimo roll in all conditions before trying surf kayaking.

# Kayak touring

Many kayakers enjoy taking long trips. Some even take camping gear with them. They camp overnight on a beach, and fall asleep listening to the sound of the water nearby.

## River and sea touring

Slow-flowing rivers and the ocean coast can both be explored in a touring kayak. The water is not as rough as in white-water rivers. This means you have time to enjoy the scenery and explore.

Kayak touring is a great way to see some fantastic scenery.

## Overnight stays

Finding a secret beach, unpacking your kayak, and setting up camp overnight is lots of fun. Just be sure that you camp far enough from the water to avoid being swept away if there is a sudden **flash flood**.

## Picking a campsite

Pick a campsite on the highest ground available. Also try to set up camp with some trees or bushes between you and the water. If they have grown there without being swept away by the water, you should stay dry overnight.

**WATCH OUT!**
Never kayak tour alone. If you get lost or find rough water, there will be no one to help.

**Top tip!**
Avoid kayaking in water where there could be alligators. They sometimes attack boats.

Pick the right campsite for a warm and dry night's sleep.

# Surf kayaking

Surf kayaking uses similar skills to white-water kayaking. Surf kayakers use the force of waves, rather than rushing rivers, to get a thrilling ride.

## Paddling out

Paddling out through breaking waves is tricky. Waves usually come in sets, or groups, of three to seven waves at a time. Paddling in the gap between sets is the best way to get to calmer water.

When paddling through white-water surf, experienced paddlers usually point their kayak straight at the waves. They paddle hard and try to punch their kayak through the white water.

Experienced surf kayakers can ride powerful waves.

## Ocean safety rules

These rules help keep the ocean safe for swimmers, kayakers, surfers, and others.

- Never go out on your own. If you or the person you are with cannot get through the breaking waves, you should both stay on the beach.
- Never catch a wave that will push you toward someone who is closer to the shore. A kayak being pushed along by a wave can easily kill someone if it hits them.
- If someone has already caught a wave or catches it closer to the curl (where it first breaks), it is their wave. Do not try to catch it.

Wave skis are a good introduction to surf kayaking.

## Kayaks and wave skis

Many surf paddlers use kayaks like those ridden in white water. Others choose to use a wave ski. This is a kayak you sit on. Your feet tuck into straps on the deck. Wave skis are good for your first taste of surf kayaking. They are easier to get back onto, if a wave knocks you off.

# Fit to paddle

Getting fit means being able to do an activity for longer and more powerfully. Paddling a raft or kayak is less tiring and easier if you are fit.

## Paddling practice

The best way to get yourself fit for paddling is to do more paddling. Do not go every day, however. It is important to get some rest to let your body recover. Always doing the same kind of training can get boring, too, so try to vary the kind of paddling you do.

### Kayak polo

Kayak polo is a bit like a game of soccer played in a swimming pool. The players paddle kayaks instead of running around. It is great practice for kayaking. There are sudden sprints, quick turns, and even Eskimo rolls if you get tipped over!

As well as being great fun, kayak polo is great training for kayaking on rivers or the sea.

## Additional training

Additional training for kayaking and rafting includes running, swimming, and cycling. Any exercise that gets you out of breath will help you paddle farther without feeling tired. Swimming in particular is useful, because you get used to being in the water.

**Top tip!**

Drink plenty of water. Experts recommend at least eight glasses a day, or more if you are doing exercise.

## Food for fitness

What you eat affects your fitness. Too many fatty foods such as burgers, fries, pizza, white bread, cake, sweets, or chocolate will not give your body the energy it needs. Instead, follow the balanced breakdown of foods shown in the pyramid below.

Eating healthy food helps you to keep fit.

MyPyramid.gov
STEPS TO A HEALTHIER YOU

This pyramid shows the balance of foods you need to stay healthy. The colors shown (from left to right) are for grains, vegetables, fruit, oils, milk, and meat and beans.

# Paddling around the world

There are great rivers, lakes, and coastlines around the world for rafters and kayakers. This is a selection of just a few.

### Alpine rivers of Europe
**Name**  The Alps
**Location**  France, Italy, Switzerland, Austria
**Description**  The Alpine rivers come alive in spring, when the snow melts and fills them with water.

### Thrills in Nepal
**Name**  Sun Kosi and Tamur rivers
**Location**  Nepal
**Description**  Waters rushing down from the world's highest mountains, the Himalayas, make for an exciting kayaking experience.

### World's widest waterfall
**Name**  Zambezi River
**Location**  Zambia
**Description**  Kayakers and rafters can begin their trip from the base of the giant Victoria Falls—the widest waterfall in the world.

## Canyon rafting

**Name**    Grand Canyon

**Location**    United States

**Description**    The world's most famous canyon is so big it can be seen from space! People spend more than a week rafting down it.

## Lakes and surf

**Name**    Myall Lakes National Park, New South Wales

**Location**    Australia

**Description**    The lakes and waterways here are great for exploring by kayak. Cross the dunes to the ocean and there are great surf kayaking beaches, too.

## For experts only!

**Name**    Patagonia

**Location**    Chile, Argentina

**Description**    Often far from help or hospitals, the rivers of Patagonia are for experts only.

## Spectacular white-water adventures

**Name**    Franklin River, Tasmania

**Location**    Australia

**Description**    The Franklin River has many white-water sections and passes through spectacular scenery. Rafting down the river can take more than a week.

# Interview: Paddle crazy!

Hamish has been kayaking since he was nine years old, and now he paddles every kind of raft and kayak he can find.

**When did you begin kayaking?**

I went on a school trip where we did all kinds of activities. One of them was kayaking. It was just in a pool, but I really enjoyed it so I bugged my mom to let me go on a proper course!

**What happened next?**

I started playing kayak polo, then began river kayaking. By the time I was 18, I was a qualified instructor.

**What was your favorite kayaking experience?**

So far, it's been kayaking in Argentina. We spent a month there last year, and the isolation of some of the places we camped was amazing.

**And what was your worst experience?**

Seeing an inexperienced kayaker nearly drown on a river in Maine. He hadn't been truthful about how experienced he was, and he tipped over at the first white water section. We only just got to him in time.

**How has kayaking changed you?**

It's allowed me to live a great outdoor life. I teach or guide kayaking trips in the spring and summer, then I teach snowboarding in winter!

# Glossary

**blades**

the wide parts at the end of paddles, that are dipped in the water and used to move a kayak or raft along

**carrying toggle**

the small handle at each end of a kayak, used for carrying or dragging it

**cockpit**

the hole on the middle of a kayak that the paddler sits inside

**cuffs**

ends of sleeves, which can be done up so that they fit more tightly on your wrists

**flash flood**

a sudden rush of lots of water along a river or riverbed

**moor**

tie a boat up to a solid object so that it cannot drift away

**puncture**

a hole that has been made in the skin of something

**rapids**

part of a river where the water is fast-moving

**stroke**

dipping the paddle in and pulling it backward to move your kayak or raft forward

**white-water rivers**

rivers with frothing water, caused when they rush over obstacles, such as rocks

# Index